Misty, the Little Furry Comfort Cat

Cat Mama Librarians Cats, Book 4

Brenda S. Parris

Misty, the Little Furry Comfort Cat
Cat Mama Librarian's Cats, Book 4

To request permissions, contact the author at bsp055@yahoo.com or sign the guestbook at https://www.zarcrom.com/users/yeartorem

ISBN: 9798994947142 (hardcover)
ISBN: 9798994947128 (paperback)
ISBN: 9798994947135 (Kindle eBook)
Back Home Books
Decatur, Alabama
backhomebooks.info
brendasparris.com

Illustrations done by the author
using ChatGPT and Canva

In memory of Angel,
who was with us only
one month after I came.
Mom says I took her place.
-- Misty

Hi, I'm Misty!
I'm a small long-haired black cat
with a very fluffy tail.

Angel saw me first, when she looked
out the living room window.
Angel was all white except just
a few black and brown spots.

I kept coming back.
Mom started feeding me.

I would come down
from the roof of the house,
onto the greenhouse ...

... then slide
down the column
on the patio.

Mom started calling me.
She gave me the name Misty
because she had looked out
and seen me out there
in the misty morning,
which she said came from a song.

Is this your cat?
found hanging around my porch. Please contact me if this is your kitty.
Post
Mom posted on Facebook
and other places online
to try to find out
who I belonged to.

Decatur
Animal Care
One day she caught me and took me to the vet. The vet asked what she wanted to do about me. Mom said "Keep her!"

So then she took me in.
She kept me in a separate
room for a couple weeks ...

then introduced me
to the others,
a little more each day.

By that time Angel's disease
started making her sick.
Mom had to give her fluids ...

... till she passed away
at the end of my first month here.

Angel had slept with Mom,
on her back.

I started doing that, and
Mom said I was sent to her,
to comfort her
after losing Angel.

Cocoa and I both sleep with Mom.
He and I love each other.
We cuddle up together a lot.

Tiger used to chase me a lot ....,

but as he's getting older
he is not so bad,
and Elsa keeps him occupied.

Elsa was afraid of me at first.
Though I am smaller,
I let her know I am not afraid of her.

Cocoa is afraid of Elsa
because she chases him.
I get between them sometimes
and try to protect
my big sweet Cocoa.

I'm glad Mom found me.
I'm very happy, so happy
sometimes I jump on her back,
but I'm so small it doesn't hurt.
I love being her comfort kitty.

It's a true story

Hi! I'm Misty's mom. I'm also mom to Cocoa, Tiger, and Elsa. My two girls and my two boys each have their own individual personalities and talents. Cocoa and Tiger have already told their stories in my series, *Cat Mama Librarian's Cats*, and in this one, Misty told her story. In the next one, Elsa will tell her story. Stay tuned, and no, she's not all bad. You will see that when you read her story.

Misty

Cocoa and Misty

Tiger and Elsa

Cocoa and Misty

Tiger and Elsa

Books about Little Black Cats

Barker, Sonny. *My Little Black Cat*. Independently Published, 2021. ISBN: 9798768795535

Creative Pages. *Luna the Little Black Cat and the Lost Bird*. (Luna the Little Black Cat's Adventures). Independently Published, 2025. ISBN: 9798297713413

Malik, Linda. *Willow's Tale: a Little Black Cat Goes a Long Way*. (Willow's Tale: the Adventures of a Little Black Cat). K. Laurit's Publishing, 2019. ISBN: 9781733049801

Manuel, G. N. *The Little Black Cat Who Reached the Stars*. Independently Published, 2026. ISBN: 9798249345822

More Books about Little Black Cats

Maya, Tara. *Little Black Cat*. Independently Published, 2012. ISBN: 9781479128129

Salvatore, Alyssa. *My Little Scaredy Cat*. Magical Black Cat, 2025. ISBN: 9798218826925

Stanley, S. E. *Two Little Black Kittens: a Bedtime Story Book*. Independently Published, 2024. ISBN: 9798878924450

Thatcher, Helen. *A Little Black Cat's Big Adventure*. Skippy Creek, 2018. ISBN: 9781945619830

Treanor, Caroline. *Calm Down Little Black Cat*. (Clever Baby Series). Caroline Treanor International Books, 2020 ISBN: 9781649706713

www.ingramcontent.com/pod-product-compliance
Lightning Source LLC
LaVergne TN
LVHW070206110826
845147LV00002B/514

* 9 7 9 8 9 9 4 9 4 7 1 2 8 *